Patterns for Devotion

PATTERNS
FOR
DEVOTION

Twenty-seven Story Worship Services

by

Gladys C. Murrell

ABINGDON PRESS
NASHVILLE   AND   NEW YORK

PATTERNS FOR DEVOTIONS

Copyright 1950 by Pierce & Smith

Library of Congress Catalog Card Number: 50-8419

"Fundamental," pp. 29-30, is from *Silver in the
Sun,* by Grace Noll Crowell, copyrighted 1956 by
Grace Noll Crowell and used by permission of the
publisher, Harper & Row.
The poem on p. 74 is from *Bound in the Bundle
of Life* by Margaret T. Applegarth, copyrighted 1941
by Harper & Brothers, used by permission of the
publisher.

PRINTED AND BOUND AT NASHVILLE,
TENNESSEE, UNITED STATES OF AMERICA

PREFACE

THIS BOOK of story worship services has been prepared for the use of those who wish to lead others in attitudes of Christian living and thinking.

These services may be adapted readily for use in various organizations and groups. They may be abbreviated or extended in length.

Thanks are due to the writers and publishers who have permitted the use of their valuable and inspiring material.

It is my prayer that other lives may be enriched by the use of these services, even as I have received a blessing in the assembling, preparation, and writing of them.

GLADYS C. MURRELL

CONTENTS

The Abiding Life

And good may ever conquer ill,
    Health walk where pain has trod;
As a man thinketh, so is he;
    Rise, then, and think with God.
              —AUTHOR UNKNOWN

SCRIPTURE: John 15:1-17.

HYMNS: "Close to Thee"; "My Jesus, as Thou Wilt."

THE STORY:

I used to wonder why a rotten apple placed in a barrel of sound apples would make the sound apples rotten, while a sound apple placed in a barrel of rotten apples would not make the rotten apples sound.

I also wondered why a man infected with smallpox when turned loose in a gathering of sound people would—by his mere presence—make many sound people sick, while a sound man walking through a hospital of sick people would not—by his mere presence—make the sick people well.

In other words, I wondered why God, if he were a good God, had made a universe in which soundness and health seemed futile and rottenness and sickness seemed contagious.

But one day I stopped wondering and examined the so-called sound apple, and I found it was not sound. It was lacerated, torn, wounded to the death.

11

Oh, I know the grocer would contradict me; he would see no defect. He might even sue me for slander if I persisted in spreading the report that he was selling apples that were not perfect.

But if he pressed me for proof, I would prove it. I would ask him to look beyond the apple to the stem. There in the most vital, the most crucial spot of all he would find the mortal wound that I refer to. He would find that the apple had been torn away from its parent stem; it had been hopelessly separated from its source of life.

When I discovered this, I learned one of the truest facts of life—that nothing, whether it be fruit, vegetable, or man, when separated from its source of life is sound.[1]

> There's part of the sun in the apple,
>   There's part of the moon in a rose;
> There's part of the flaming Pleiades
>   In every leaf that grows.
>
> Out of the vast comes nearness;
>   For the God whose love we sing
> Lends a little of his heaven
>   To every living thing.
>   —AUGUST WRIGHT BAMBERGER

PRAYER:

Our Father God, grant that thy will may be our guide, that we may never choose aside from thee, that thy will may be our purpose, our strength, our inspiration, and our hope. Give us faith, constancy, and perseverance, that we may be numbered rightly in thy holy family. Amen.

I IN THEE AND THOU IN ME

I am but clay in thy hands; but thou art the all-loving
   artist;
   Passive I live in thy sight, yet in my selfhood I strive
So to embody the life and love thou ever impartest
   That in my spheres of the finite I may be truly alive.

Knowing thou needest this form, as I thy divine
   inspiration,
   Knowing thou shapest the clay with a vision and
   purpose divine,
So would I answer each touch of thy hand in its loving
   creation,
   That in my conscious life thy power and beauty may
   shine.

. . . .

So in thy love will I trust, bringing me sooner or later
   Past the dark screen that divides these shows of the
   finite from thee.
Thine, thine only, this warm dear life, O loving Creator!
   Thine the invisible future, born of the present, must be.
                                   —CHRISTOPHER PEARSE CRANCH [2]

Beginning Again

I give the life Thou gavest,
  My present, future, past;
My joys, my fears, my sorrows,
  My first hope and my last.
                    —AUTHOR UNKNOWN

SCRIPTURE: Philippians 4:13; 3:12-16.

HYMNS: "My Jesus, as Thou Wilt"; "More Love to Thee, O Christ."

THE STORY:

Quentin Matsys was a Flemish painter who died about four hundred years ago. When he was a young man, he was an apprentice to a blacksmith and became an excellent workman. He loved the beautiful and in his leisure time created artistic pieces of ironwork for his own pleasure.

The daughter of an artist, a beautiful girl, paused one day at the door of his shop to examine a piece of his work. He saw her and came out to explain it to her. There he stood in his leather apron, with dirty face and hands, beside the delicately gowned girl. And there he fell in love with her. He knew she was not attracted to him, but he decided to wait upon her father to learn if he might call upon her.

Of course the father was horrified to think of a common blacksmith courting his daughter and told

14

him that only an artist of ability would be welcome in their home.

As a suitor to the girl Matsys might have been discouraged. But not he! He began his life all over again. Determining to win her hand, he gave up the forge and entered an art studio as an apprentice.

Strangely, his devotion to his work, his humble obedience to Christ, and his love for the girl awoke unexpected talent in him. His master found that he had unusual ability as a painter, and his became one of the greatest names in Flemish art. It is said by one authority that he was the first painter to run completely through the gamut of human feelings and emotions. He was a superb colorist.

Matsys always signed his pictures with three words, "As I can." This recalls the words of Jesus concerning the woman who anointed him, "She hath done what she could."

PRAYER:

O God, help us to see the greatness and wisdom of all thy ways. Open our eyes to our own possibilities and inspire us to use our talents so that we do not waste them.

Hasten the day when race, pride, and class consciousness shall vanish from the world and when good will and appreciation of all the human family shall prevail.

Forgive us our prejudices, our narrowness, and our

selfish ways. Help us to begin again and lead lives
of unselfish service. Amen.

THE LAND OF BEGINNING AGAIN

I wish that there were some wonderful place
    In the Land of Beginning Again:
Where all our mistakes and all our heartaches
    And all of our poor selfish grief
Could be dropped like a shabby old coat at the door
    And never put on again.

I wish we could come on it all unaware,
    Like the hunter who finds a lost trail;
And I wish that the one whom our blindness had done
    The greatest injustice of all
Could be there at the gates like an old friend that waits
    For the comrade he's gladdest to hail.

We would find all the things we intended to do
    But forgot, and remembered too late,
Little praises unspoken, little promises broken,
    And all of the thousand and one
Little duties neglected that might have perfected
    The day for one less fortunate.

It wouldn't be possible not to be kind
    In the Land of Beginning Again,
And the ones we misjudged and the ones whom we
    grudged
    Their moments of victory here,
Would find in the grasp of our loving hand-clasp
    More than penitent lips could explain.

For what had been hardest we'd know had been best,
    And what had seemed loss would be gain;

16

For there isn't a sting that will not take wing
   When we've faced it and laughed it away
And I think that the laughter is most what we're after
   In the Land of Beginning Again.

So I wish that there were some wonderful place
   Called the Land of Beginning Again,
Where all our mistakes and all our heartaches,
   And all of our poor selfish grief
Could be dropped like a shabby old coat at the door
   And never put on again.

—LOUISA FLETCHER TARKINGTON

The Bible

Within that awful volume lies
The mystery of mysteries!
Happiest they of human race,
To whom God has granted grace
To read, to fear, to hope, to pray,
To lift the latch, and force the way;
And better had they ne'er been born,
Who read to doubt, or read to scorn.
—SIR WALTER SCOTT

SCRIPTURE: II Timothy 3:16.

HYMNS: "Wonderful Words of Life"; "I Love to Tell the Story."

THE STORY:

One day the Bible, the Book of Books, disappeared. Not only was the book itself gone, but everything which it had influenced was not to be found. There was no record left to show that it had existed—none at all.

A strange thing became apparent everywhere. At the art galleries most of the golden frames were empty, for the great artists had been inspired by the Book.

At the libraries all writings of noble inspiration were gone. Books of poetry, drama, and all literature were almost unintelligible since all references inspired by and contained in the Bible had vanished.

All documents, statements of human rights and liberty, were unreadable. Even some lawbooks were denuded of meaning.

When people tried to express themselves, they stuttered and became dumb.

The schools, hospitals, and institutions of mercy were closed. Churches and missions no longer existed.

Human conscience knew no restraint, and life became cheap.

But this is only a dream which might become a reality. If you and I should forget to read our Bibles, and if writers, artists, and national leaders should pass aside the principles taught in the Book of Books, this could happen here.

The ideals of living enshrined in the Bible lie buried unless they are lived again in each generation.

PRAYER:

Our Father God, we thank thee for the Book of Books and for thy inspiration which has preserved and protected these writings through many thousands of years.

Help us to be mindful of the many who have sacrificed that this book might live for us.

May we avail ourselves of the privileges which are ours today and become more familiar with our Bible so that its teachings may be truly written on our hearts. Amen.

THE ANVIL—GOD'S WORD

Last eve I passed beside a blacksmith's door,
    And heard the anvil ring the vesper chime;
Then looking in, I saw upon the floor
    Old hammers, worn with beating years of time.

"How many anvils have you had," said I,
    "To wear and batter all these hammers so?"
"Just one," said he, and then, with twinkling eye,
    "The anvil wears the hammers out, you know."

And so, thought I, the anvil of God's word,
    For ages skeptic blows have beat upon;
Yet, though the noise of falling blows was heard,
    The anvil is unharmed—the hammers gone.

                —JOHN CLIFFORD

Blessings

No service in itself is small;
  None great, though earth it fill;
But that is small that seeks its own,
  And great that seeks God's will.
  —AUTHOR UNKNOWN

SCRIPTURE: James 1:19-26.

HYMNS: "O Master, Let Me Walk with Thee";
"Work, for the Night Is Coming"; "Go, Labor On."

THE STORY:

There was a rap at my kitchen door one warm
July morning, and an old crippled umbrella mender
stood there, smiling at me. With mending kit upon
his back he balanced himself neatly on his crutch as
he cheerfully solicited work.

Arranging a seat for him, I asked if he wished a
table or bench upon which to work.

"Oh, no," he said, as he grinned broadly. "I place
my crutch across my lap for a table. You see, I am
luckier than most traveling workmen; all of them
don't have crutches."

I left him to go on with his work, but with a lift
of spirit as I reviewed my own blessings. Sometimes
I had complained because of the limitations of my
life. Now I saw it full of possibilities and privileges.

Then I heard the old man singing hymns—"How Happy Every Child of Grace" and "Blessed Assurance."

As I had been working about my pleasant kitchen early in the morning, I had been wrapped in gloomy thoughts. But now I joined my voice to that of the old umbrella mender, and I trust that if anyone heard us that July morning, he too caught a blessing.

PRAYER:

A WOMAN'S PRAYER

O Lord, thou knowest every need of mine;
Help me to bear each cross and not repine;
    Grant me fresh courage every day;
    Help me to do my work alway
        Without complaint!

O Lord, thou knowest well how dark the way;
Guide thou my footsteps lest they stray;
    Give me fresh faith for every hour,
    Lest I should ever doubt thy power
        And make complaint!

Give me a heart, O Lord, strong to endure;
Help me to keep it simple, pure;
    Make me unselfish, helpful, true,
    In every act whate'er I do,
        And keep content!

Help me to do my woman's share;
Make me courageous, strong to bear
    Sunshine or shadow in my life;
    Sustain me in the daily strife
        To keep content.   Amen.
              —AUTHOR UNKNOWN

MY SERVICE

I asked the Lord to let me do
  Some mighty work for Him;
To fight amid His battle hosts,
  Then sing the victor's hymn.
I longed my ardent love to show,
But Jesus would not have it so.

He placed me in a quiet home,
  Whose life was calm and still,
And gave me little things to do,
  My daily round to fill;
I could not think it good to be
Just put aside so silently.

Small duties gathered round my way,
  They seemed of earth alone;
I, who had longed for conquests bright
  To lay before His throne,
Had common things to do and bear,
To watch and strive with daily care.

So then I thought my prayer unheard,
  And asked the Lord once more
That He would give me work for Him
  And open wide the door;
Forgetting that my Master knew
Just what was best for me to do.

Then quietly the answer came,
  "My child, I hear thy cry;
Think not that mighty deeds alone
  Will bring the victory,
The battle has been planned by Me;
Let daily life thy conquests see."
                    —Author Unknown

23

True Brotherhood

God, what a world, if men in street and mart
Felt that same kinship of the human heart
Which makes them, in the face of fire and flood,
Rise to the meaning of True Brotherhood.
—ELLA WHEELER WILCOX[3]

SCRIPTURE: John 13:34-35.

HYMNS: "A Charge to Keep I Have"; "O Jesus, I Have Promised."

THE STORY:

Once there lived a prince who was very sad. He had toys, money, books, and plenty to eat and to wear. Everyone was kind to him. He did not know why he was unhappy.

One day he went to his father, the king. "Father," he asked, "why are you so happy?"

"Well," said the king, "I guess it's because I'm so busy being king that I have no time to waste."

"Busy people are happy," said the prince. "I must work!"

So he got a garden spade and hoe and worked until night. But he was not happy—only tired.

Then he went to the king's treasurer.

"Tell me, please, why are you so happy?"

24

"I guess it's because I save the king's money for him," answered the king's treasurer.

"Saving! That is the secret," said the prince.

So for a week he did not spend a penny, but still remained very sad. Then he went to the man who paid the king's bills.

"Tell me, please, why are you happy when I am so sad?" he asked.

"I guess it's because I enjoy spending money," replied the man, smiling.

"Spending! That's what makes people happy," said the prince.

So he took all the money out of his bank and went out to buy things. But he didn't know where to put them, and he was sadder than before.

He decided then to walk by himself outside the palace grounds. So he slipped quietly through the big gate.

At last he came to a small boy who was crying. As the prince stood there, a big boy came up to where they were.

"What is wrong, sonny?" he asked.

"My kite will not fly; it just spins around and comes down quickly."

"It needs more tail," said the big boy. "Let me help you."

He fastened some pieces of paper to the tail of the kite and held it as high as he could against the wind. The little boy grabbed the string and ran fast. The kite was in the air, and it was holding steady.

Then the big boy smiled at the little boy and at the prince, as he walked away whistling. Catching up with him, the prince asked, "Why are you so happy?"

"Because I forget myself and try to make others happy," answered the big boy.

"That," thought the prince, "is the real answer to my question." And it was!

PRAYER:

Give me, O God, the understanding heart—
    The quick discernment of the soul to see
Another's inner wish, the hidden part
    Of him who, wordless, speaks for sympathy.
I would be kind, but kindness is not all:
    In arid places may I find the wells,
The deeps within my neighbor's soul that call
    To me, and lead me where his spirit dwells.
When Jesus lifted Mary Magdalene,
    And Mary came with alabaster cruse,
A deed was wrought—but more; that there was seen
    The bond of holy love of which I muse.
Give me, O God, the understanding heart,
Lit with the quickening flame Thou dost impart. Amen.
                                —GEORGIA HARKNESS [4]

NOT LOST

The look of sympathy; the gentle word
Spoken so low that only angels heard;
The secret act of pure self-sacrifice,
    Unseen by men, but marked by angels' eyes—
        These are not lost.

The happy dreams that gladdened all our youth
When dreams had less of self and more of truth;
The childhood's faith, so tranquil and so sweet,
Which sat like Mary at the Master's feet;
      These are not lost.

The kindly plans devised for others' good,
So seldom guessed, so little understood;
The quiet, steadfast love that strove to win
Some weary wanderer from the ways of sin—
      These are not lost.

—SARAH DOUDNEY

The Christian Home

It is time to become little children once more, to learn that what we know is but a trifle.

SCRIPTURE: Proverbs 31:10-23; Matthew 19:13-15; 18:5, 6-10.

HYMNS: "Tell Me the Stories of Jesus"; "I Think When I Read That Sweet Story."

THE STORY:

One day a young mother went gloomily about the house performing her tasks. She made the beds with many groans; she washed the dishes noisily and swept the floors with desperate strokes of the broom.

Her five-year-old daughter followed her quietly but with sad little sighs. Finally she asked, "Mother, what hurts you?"

"Oh, nothing much," the mother answered, "but I did want to go to that party today, and I have nothing fit to wear."

The child was silent for a while; then she left the room and went to a little box in which lay twenty-five cents, which she had been saving to buy a doll. Hurrying back, she cried, "Guess what I have?"

The mother's face brightened at her child's happiness. "Something nice, I am sure," she said, smiling.

28

The little girl laughed aloud and, opening her hand, showed a shiny quarter.

"Now you can get a dress and go to the party!" she cried gleefully.

The young mother knelt and kissed the child. "Come, darling," she said. "Our work is finished for today."

They dressed in clean dresses. Mother fixed the picnic basket after making a telephone call to her husband.

As they started out together down the street, the child asked, "Are we both going to the party, Mother?"

"Yes, we are both going to our very own party in the park," laughed the young mother, "and Daddy will join us for picnic supper."

"Hurrah!" said the little girl.

"Hurrah!" said the young mother. The world was a happy place again.

FUNDAMENTAL

"What makes a home?"
I asked my little boy,
And this is what he said,
"You, Mother,
And when Father comes,
Our table set all shiny,
And my bed,
And, Mother, I think it's home,
Because we love each other."

You who are old and wise,
What would you say

29

If you were asked the question?
Tell me, pray.
And simply as a little child,
The old wise ones can answer nothing more.
A man, a woman, and a child,
Their love,
Warm as the gold hearth fire along the floor.
A table, and a lamp for light,
And smooth white beds at night.
Only the old, sweet fundamental things.

And long ago I learned—
Home may be near; home may be far,
But it is anywhere that love
And a few plain household treasures are.

—GRACE NOLL CROWELL

PRAYER:

Father of all mankind, we thank thee for the simple faith of little children, remembering that thy Son once said to his disciples, "Except ye become as little children, ye shall not enter into the kingdom of heaven."

May we never fail these little ones in patient understanding and wisdom as they turn to us for guidance.

Bless all efforts that are made in behalf of child welfare and wipe out from the souls of all neglected children the scars of fear and suffering. Help us to do our part in giving back to them the untroubled joy which should be theirs. In thy Son's name. Amen.

Christmas

Only a manger, cold and bare,
  Only a maiden mild,
Only some shepherds kneeling there,
  Watching a little Child;
And yet that maiden's arms enfold
  The King of Heaven above;
And in the Christ-Child we behold
  The Lord of Life and Love.

—Author Unknown

Scripture: Luke 2:1-20.

Hymns: "Away in a Manger"; "Silent Night"; "There's a Song in the Air."

The Story:

The carpenter's shop in Nazareth was quiet. The young boy and his father worked skillfully side by side, with no words wasted.

Joseph's wife, Mary, and the small children had gone to the well for water. As she would be away for an hour, for she often lingered to talk with the other women, Jesus brought out the chest which he and Joseph were making as a surprise for Mary.

Each year it was so—a gift was made by Jesus to be presented to his mother on his birthday. From the time he was a little boy he had made a special gift for her each year. To be sure, Joseph took great

31

delight in helping him and in keeping the secret, but the design and plan were Jesus' own.

Between his mother and her oldest son there was an understanding, shared by Joseph. The story of Jesus' birth had been told often by his mother. Her eyes dwelt wonderingly upon him as she related the unusual events which were a part of that night in Bethlehem. Always a wistful sadness settled over the listening group, but there was a feeling too of hope and the promise of something not fully understood.

To Jesus his birthday was a special day, and no sacrifice was too great to make for his mother's happiness.

This chest was a marvel of workmanship. There was no metal used in it, but the wood was so beautifully shaped and fitted together that it would seemingly last forever. The carving upon it was a thing of beauty in which Jesus had symbolized his love and understanding. On the top of the chest appeared a single star which shed its long slender rays to every corner of the lid. Around the right side of the chest came the shepherds and the sheep, on the left side the wise men on their camels, and on the front of the chest was the cave, the manger, and the child, brooded over by Mary and Joseph. The animals were resting quietly on the floor.

This was to be the finest gift of all, and Joseph was proud of the boy, who was also his right-hand helper in the carpenter shop. How he had conceived and planned this exquisite piece of carving was a wonder and delight to Joseph. The other articles of woodwork about the shop were plain and, though substantially and honestly designed and made, they were sadly out of spirit with this living testament of love and devotion.

The chest was almost completed, with the design made and the carving under way. With swift, certain movements of the knife Jesus worked in the heat of the small shop.

Suddenly he heard an unusual sound and looking around saw that Joseph had slumped down upon the floor. Quickly dropping his work, he hastened for water and, resting the sick man upon a pallet, tried to ease his pain. Then he heard his mother and the other children coming. The father roused and called weakly, "Cover the chest; she must not see it until it is finished." Then with one quick movement Jesus pushed the chest into a corner, covering it with coarse sackcloth.

The days that followed were full of toil and responsibility for all the family. The father was ill for many months, and the young man took upon himself the care of the household. He filled the orders for ox yokes, benches, tables, and grain bins, working early and late. Then Joseph died.

Many years of devoted companionship Jesus gave to the little family, but year by year the other children were trained to do their part.

Now and then Jesus found a few moments to work upon the chest which he had started so many years ago. As his thirtieth birthday drew near, the carving was finished. The completing of this labor of love seemed to him also a symbol of his release from responsibility to his brothers and sisters and the call to a wider ministry. The children were now old enough to care for Mary and to manage the carpenter shop.

On his birthday morning very early he heard his mother moving about and went to tell her of his decision. She had already sensed what was in his mind and knew that God was calling him to his appointed task.

And so they parted for a while—Jesus to his active life of ministry and Mary to discover the chest which brought to her mind the story of his miraculous birth. Each time she looked at it Mary felt his love and loyalty, and never did she doubt his divine call.

IN THE CARPENTER SHOP

I wish I had been His apprentice,
  To see Him each morning at seven,
As he tossed His gray tunic about Him,
  The Master of earth and of heaven;
When He lifted the lid of His work chest
  And opened His carpenter's kit,
And looked at His chisels and augers,
  And took the bright tools out of it;
When He gazed at the rising sun tinting
  The dew on the opening flowers,
And He smiled at the thought of His Father
  Whose love floods this fair world of ours;
When He fastened the apron about Him,
  And put on His workingman's cap,

And grasped the smooth haft of His hammer
  To give the bent woodwork a tap,
Saying, "Lad, let us finish this ox yoke,
  The farmer must finish his crop."
Oh, I wish I had been His apprentice
  And worked in the Nazareth shop.
                —Author Unknown

PRAYER:

Giver of all gifts, we pray that thy Spirit may descend upon our hearts this Christmas season.

Help us to put aside all prejudices and vainglory and to become merciful, understanding, and loving. Amen.

HOW FAR TO BETHLEHEM

"How far is it to Bethlehem town?"
Just over Jerusalem hills adown,
Past lovely Rachel's white-domed tomb—
Sweet shrine of motherhood's young doom.

It isn't far to Bethlehem town—
Just over the dusty roads adown,
Past Wise Men's well, still offering
Cool draughts from welcome wayside spring;
Past shepherds with their flutes of reed
That charm the woolly sheep they lead;
Past boys with kites on hilltops flying,
And soon you're there where Bethlehem's lying.
Sunned white and sweet on olived slopes,
Gold-lighted still with Judah's hopes.

And so we find the Shepherd's field
And plain that gave rich Boaz yield;

35

And look where Herod's villa stood.
We thrill that earthly parenthood
Could foster Christ who was all-good;
And thrill that Bethlehem town today
Looks down on Christian homes that pray.

It isn't far to Bethlehem town!
It's anywhere that Christ comes down
And finds in people's friendly face
A welcome and abiding place.
The road to Bethlehem runs right through
The homes of folks like me and you.
    —MADELEINE SWEENEY MILLER [5]

Contentment

Diving, and finding no pearls in the sea,
Blame not the ocean; the fault is in thee!
—FROM THE PERSIAN

SCRIPTURE: I Timothy 6:6-8; Philippians 4:11-13; Malachi 3:10.

HYMNS: "Lord of Life and King of Glory"; "Happy the Home When God Is There"; "How Happy Every Child of Grace."

THE STORY:

All day long the little boy worked hard, in field and barn and shed, for his people were poor farmers, and could not pay a workman; but at sunset there came an hour that was all his own, for his father had given it to him. Then the boy would go up to the top of a hill and look across at another hill that rose some miles away. On this far hill stood a house with windows of clear gold and diamonds. They shone and blazed so that it made the boy wink to look at them; but after a while the people in the house put up shutters, as it seemed, and then it looked like any common farmhouse. The boy supposed they did this because it was supper-time; and then he would go into the house and have his supper of bread and milk, and go to bed.

One day the boy's father called to him and said: "You have been a good boy, and have earned a holiday. Take this day for your own; but remember that God gave it, and try to learn some good thing."

The boy thanked his father and kissed his mother; then he put a piece of bread in his pocket, and started off to find the house with the golden windows.

It was pleasant walking. His bare feet made marks in the white dust, and when he looked back, the footprints seemed to be following him, and making company for him. His shadow, too, kept beside him, and would dance or run with him as he pleased; so it was very cheerful.

By and by he felt hungry; and he sat down by a brown brook that ran through the alder hedge by the roadside, and ate his bread, and drank the clear water. Then he scattered the crumbs for the birds, as his mother had taught him to do, and went on his way.

After a long time he came to a high green hill; and when he had climbed the hill, there was the house on the top; but it seemed that the shutters were up, for he could not see the golden windows. He came up to the house, and then he could well have wept, for the windows were of clear glass, like any others, and there was no gold anywhere about them.

A woman came to the door, and looked kindly at the boy, and asked him what he wanted.

"I saw the golden windows from our hilltop," he

said, "and I came to see them, but now they are only glass."

The woman shook her head and laughed.

"We are poor farming people," she said, "and are not likely to have gold about our windows; but glass is better to see through."

She bade the boy sit down on the broad stone step at the door, and brought him a cup of milk and a cake, and bade him rest; then she called her daughter, a child of his own age, and nodded kindly at the two, and went back to her work.

The little girl was barefooted like himself, and wore a brown cotton gown, but her hair was golden like the windows he had seen, and her eyes were blue like the sky at noon. She led the boy about the farm, and showed him her black calf with the white star on its forehead, and he told her about his own at home, which was red like a chestnut, with four white feet. Then when they had eaten an apple together, and so had become friends, the boy asked her about the golden windows. The little girl nodded, and said she knew all about them, only he had mistaken the house.

"You have come the wrong way!" she said. "Come with me, and I will show you the house with the golden windows, and then you will see for yourself."

They went to a knoll that rose behind the farmhouse, and as they went the little girl told him that the golden windows could only be seen at a certain hour, about sunset.

"Yes, I know that!" said the boy.

When they reached the top of the knoll, the girl turned and pointed; and there on a hill far away stood a house with windows of clear gold and diamond, just as he had seen them. And when they looked again, the boy saw that it was his own home.

Then he told the little girl that he must go; and he gave her his best pebble, the white one with the red band, that he had carried for a year in his pocket; and she gave him three horse-chestnuts, one red like satin, one spotted, and one white like milk. He kissed her, and promised to come again, but he did not tell her what he had learned; and so he went back down the hill, and the little girl stood in the sunset light and watched him.

The way home was long, and it was dark before the boy reached his father's house; but the lamplight and firelight shone through the windows, making them almost as bright as he had seen them from the hilltop; and when he opened the door, his mother came to kiss him, and his little sister ran to throw her arms about his neck, and his father looked up and smiled from his seat by the fire.

"Have you had a good day?" asked his mother.

Yes, the boy had had a very good day.

"And have you learned anything?" asked his father.

"Yes!" said the boy. "I have learned that our house has windows of gold and diamond." •

PRAYER:

Our heavenly Father, who hast created the earth to be our home, forgive us for our vain strivings for material things.

Grant that through thy mercy we may see beauty in all the common things of our lives, that the golden windows and green pastures of the distance may not lure us from the joy in everyday living and the daily acknowledgment of thy great gifts to us.

Light our minds and spirits with vision, perspective, and appreciation, that we may rejoice in the wholesome ways of everyday life.

Bless those who lack the common necessities and inspire us to do our part to make possible a better situation for them. In Jesus' name. Amen.

THE OTHER FELLOW'S JOB

There's a craze among us mortals that is cruel hard to name;
Wheresoe'er you find a human, you will find the case the same;
You may seek among the worst of men or seek among the best,
And you'll find that every person is precisely like the rest:
Each believes his real calling is along some other line
Than the one at which he's working—take, for instance, yours and mine.
From the meanest "me-too" creature to the leader of the mob,
There's a universal craving for "the other fellow's job."

There are millions of positions in the busy world today,
Each a drudge to him who holds it, but to him who
   doesn't, play;
Every farmer's brokenhearted that in youth he missed
   his call,
While that same unhappy farmer is the envy of us all.
Any task you care to mention seems a vastly better lot
Than the one especial something which you happen to
   have got.
There's but one sure way to smother Envy's heartache
   and her sob:
Keep too busy at your own to want "the other fellow's
   job."

—STRICKLAND W. GILLILAN [7]

Courage

Shallow water is not for diving;
  Never leap in a shallow stream.
Green ocean depths are for your striving;
  Deep, deep down is a world of dream.

Shallow lives are not for living;
  Swim where the rough waves surge and leap.
Life is not taking; life is giving;
  Plunge where the currents are strong and deep.
  —Charles Hanson Towne [8]

Scripture: Proverbs 31:25-31.

Hymns: "In the Hour of Trial"; "My Soul, Be on Thy Guard."

The Story:

A woman who was faced with tuberculosis was sent to a sanatorium in the mountains. At first she felt she was in a prison and would never get well.

As she looked across to another bed, she saw the face of a Chinese girl and began to realize that she knew nothing about people of other races and countries. Since talking was not allowed in this room of rest, she asked for a book about China.

Then she decided that, though she must leave all her customary friends and be inactive physically for a while, she could still travel in her mind to places

43

she had never hoped to go. She asked for books and magazines of travel and made out an itinerary. Becoming familiar with the characteristics and customs of people in faraway places occupied her for many months. She wrote letters to friends she had never seen. She learned to understand people in many lands better. The woman began to be grateful for the many blessings which came to her because she lived in America. With gratefulness she regained her health. She went home with the realization that her illness marked the beginning of a grand adventure in understanding and appreciating the blessings of God.

When life seems very narrow and very small, God has given us a way of growth through our imagination and through our ability to learn. There are many perplexing situations, many choices, decisions, and opportunities for action on our part. Some few may give up and lose heart, but others will apply themselves to the solution to these problems. When we learn to face afflictions squarely and to solve our difficulties with intelligence, we are on our way toward becoming adult.

Our lives may be like the bishop's garden, "very narrow and very short but very high."

PRAYER:

Dear Father, lead us deeper into life, into companionship with all who live. Give us vision and perspective when the curtain of sorrow or illness seems to close around us. May we thrust it aside and use our imagination to broaden our view. Realizing that in quiet and loneliness often comes an opportunity for spiritual growth, we thank thee for these times. May we use them wisely. In Jesus name we ask it. Amen.

MY SPIRIT WILL GROW UP

Some day my spirit will grow up tall and wise,
And then, stern Life, I shall no longer go
Cowardly running and crying from your blow.
Then I will face you with clear, earnest eyes
Smiling a little at your sharp surprise,
Unflinching from the threatened stroke, with no
Soft tremor to lighten your frown—when I shall grow
In spirit, some day, tall and strong and wise.
Then I will face you; it may be I shall laugh,
Not to disarm you, not to conclude our strife,
But joyous in my newly steadied will
That finds a comfort in thy rod and staff.
Then I will say: "You may hurt me, hurt me, Life,
Hurt me your worst, and I will love you still!"
                    —RUTH EVELYN HENDERSON

Duty

I slept, and dreamed that life was Beauty;
I woke, and found that life was Duty.
—ELLEN STURGIS HOOPER

SCRIPTURE: Luke 15:3-10.

HYMNS: "Pass Me Not, O Gentle Saviour"; "I Need Thee Every Hour."

THE STORY:

Susanna stood by the side of the road watching the people pass. She wondered why so many were walking along the king's highway.

Finally she called out to Ruth, her friend, whom she recognized in the throng, "Where are you going?"

"Oh, don't you know? The king has lost his royal ruby," replied Ruth.

"Where did he lose it?"

"No one knows! He attended a banquet and wore it on his golden chain. Everyone is hunting along the highway, where he traveled in his royal coach. Come along!"

"But I cannot go without asking Mother," called Susanna.

"And I cannot wait. I may find the ruby. The king has offered a bag of gold as a reward." So Ruth hurried on.

Susanna ran home and told her mother about the search, but her mother shook her head sadly.

"Dear child," she answered, "you must watch the sheep. Your father is away, and there is no one to take them down by the brook to graze."

So Susanna's dancing feet slowed themselves to the pace of the sheep and lambs as she led them to the pasture and the stream.

She thought of the joy of returning the gem to the king and of the rewarding bag of gold with which many needed things could be purchased by her mother.

But she was kind and gentle to the stupid, bleating animals, and when the sun grew hot, she led them to the cool water. Sitting on the bank, she was aware of a sparkle in the stream. What was it? Leaping up, she reached out her eager fingers and touched a ruby surrounded by pearls and diamonds formed into the royal crest.

"The King's jewel!" she cried. "The brook has carried it to this bank. It must have fallen as he crossed the bridge on the highway."

While the sheep drank the cool water, she ran swiftly home to tell her mother the news. As her mother clasped her in her arms, she said quietly, "We shall rejoice with all your friends because of your loyalty to duty and because of the return of the lost jewel to the king."

Susanna never forgot this lesson.

47

PRAYER:

Dear Father, we thank thee for the responsibilities and duties of everyday life. May we accept them joyfully and discharge them faithfully. We ask thy watchful, purposeful guidance through our days, that we may not stumble or fail in the tasks which are ours. Amen.

WORK

Let me but do my work from day to day,
   In field or forest, at the desk or loom,
   In roaring market-place or tranquil room;
Let me but find it in my heart to say,
When vagrant wishes beckon me astray,
   "This is my work; my blessing, not my doom;
   Of all who live, I am the one by whom
This work can best be done in the right way."

Then shall I see it not too great, nor small,
   To suit my spirit and to prove my powers;
   Then shall I cheerful greet the labouring hours,
And cheerful turn, when the long shadows fall
At eventide, to play and love and rest,
Because I know for me my work is best.
              —HENRY VAN DYKE[0]

Endurance

The wind that blows can never kill
  The tree God plants;
It bloweth east; it bloweth west;
The tender leaves have little rest,
But any wind that blows is best.
  The tree God plants
Strikes deeper root, grows higher still,
Spreads wider boughs, for God's good will
  Meets all its wants.
                    —LILLIAN E. BARR

SCRIPTURE: Daniel 4:10-12; Revelation 2:7; 22:2-14; Psalm 104:6-24.

HYMNS: "From Every Stormy Wind That Blows"; "Dear Lord and Father of Mankind"; "O for a Heart of Calm Repose."

THE STORY:

He was a maker of violins. He made his living by another vocation, but he found expression for his genius by making violins. He not only made them, but played them so well that few men in all the mountain country could release such singing music.

"Where do you get the wood you use in the violins?" someone asked one day.

"At first I went to the woodyards and looked for logs of hardwood," he answered, "wood from the

49

southlands and from over the many seas. Always, when a violin was finished, some quality of tone had eluded me. Now I have found it. This one is made from wood at timberline. Timberline! The last stand of trees—twelve thousand feet into the heavens, where trees take on strange shapes, where timberline gives them personality. This one is of timberline spruce. It has resonance."

Tears came to our eyes as he played. Our nerves tingled. Resonance from timberline! Those of us who knew timberline heard again the wind as it blows up there. We had seen storms blown from the clouds; branches of trees tossed about like feathers. We had seen trees bent to their knees, their branches torn asunder with ice and sleet. They were the heroes of a high country. Easy living did not put resonance into the wood that became the perfect violin.

Easy living never puts resonance into our lives. Dread not your timberline. God can make use of it.[10]

PRAYER:

O thou who givest us life, with all its pain and possibilities, we thank thee for human love which can heal the hurt of the world. We give thanks for all pioneers and prophets who have sacrificially lived and gallantly died.

We praise thee for those of vision, who, having not met their goals, have been links in the great chain of service which in thy name binds together the world. Amen.

THE A B C'S IN GREEN

The trees are God's great alphabet:
With them He writes in shining green
Across the world His thoughts serene.

He scribbles poems against the sky
With a gay, leafy lettering,
For us and for our bettering.

The wind pulls softly at His page,
And every star and bird
Repeats in dutiful delight His word,
And every blade of grass
Flutters to class.

Like a slow child that does not heed,
I stand at summer's knees,
And from the primer of the wood
I spell that life and love are good,
I learn to read.

LEONORA SPEYER [11]

First Things First

Growing up is more than blowing out
One more birthday candle every year.
It's learning beyond doubt
That many little things which once seemed very dear
Are valueless—that you yourself are somewhat less
Than perfect—that the greatest measure
Of happiness
Is weighed in giving other people pleasure.
                    —BEULAH FRANCES HOLLAND [12]

SCRIPTURE: Proverbs 15:1-4; 3:13-20.

HYMNS: "O Sometimes the Shadows Are Deep"; "I Am Coming to the Cross."

THE STORY:

Sadie Virginia Smithson was an unknown, drab-looking seamstress, who lived in Johnson Falls, Virginia, just prior to the First World War. She had grown up in Johnson Falls. The deepest disappointment in her life was her discovery when she reached young girlhood that she was not acceptable to the social set of her town. Her one absorbing ambition to belong to the Laurel Literary Society had been frustrated. Because her father kept a stable and she sewed clothes for a living, she wasn't "elite" enough for the ladies of the Laurel Society.

So Sadie lived under the compulsion of one dominating obsession. She would scrape and save until it became possible for her to visit Europe. No one from Johnson Falls had ever gone to Europe. Surely after her return the Laurel Society would invite her to speak and perhaps even to be a member.

By 1914 Sadie had saved enough. She went to Europe and was caught in Belgium when the war broke out. An army officer offered to drive her and her party to Paris; they accepted. On the way they lost the road, and just before nightfall they found themselves crossing a battlefield shortly after a major battle had moved on.

At the side of a car Sadie saw a young soldier whose arm had been torn away, moaning, "Water! For God's sake, water!"

Almost before she knew what she was doing, Sadie jumped out of the car and brought water from a near-by spring in her collapsible drinking cup for the soldier and for dozens of others. She wandered far from the car, which finally went on and left her to spend the whole night on the battlefield with the dying and wounded boys. She bound them up with bandages torn from her skirts. She tramped back and forth to the spring. She scribbled messages and notes to the loved ones of the dying soldiers.

The first faint glimmer of dawn brought an ambulance and a young doctor, who looked at her in amazement. "Who are you, and what are you doing here?"

She calmly replied, "I am Sadie Smithson of Johnson Falls, Virginia."

As she told her almost incredible story weeks later to a shipboard friend on her way back to this country, the friend remarked, "Well, the Laurel Literary Society surely will be glad enough to have you for a member now."

The little seamstress looked puzzled for just a moment, then managed to stammer, "But you don't understand! I've been face to face with war and death and God. I've been born again. Do you think any of those little things matter now?"

"What does matter?" asked her companion.

"Nothing," she replied. "Nothing but God and love and doing things for folks." [13]

DWELL DEEP

Dwell deep! The little things that chafe and fret,
  O waste not golden hours to give them heed!
The slight, the thoughtless wrong, do thou forget,
  Be self-forgot in serving others' need.
Thou faith in God through love for man shall keep.
  Dwell deep, my soul, dwell deep.
—JAMES BUCKHAM

PRAYER:

Our heavenly Father, the little prayers of every day seem so small when we consider thy great creation and thy desires for thy children of all the ages.

Wilt thou help us to have a measure of thy patience and understanding so that petty annoyances

may be put in their proper places and that we may
be unselfish, humble, and kind. Amen.

MOMENTS

We live in moments—shining moments only,
That prick the drab fabric of our existence
As stars pierce the night.
Moments of beauty and high adventure;
Moments when we glimpse life's meaning—
An endless quest, a making of new goals,
Never an arriving.
Moments of love and understanding,
Courage, honor, dedication,
Kindness, and generosity.
Moments when we can shout for the joys of mere living.
Moments of satisfaction in life's common experiences—
In the family, in friendship, in work,
In the enjoyment of art and the out-of-doors;
Thank God for our radiant moments!
                              —CHARLOTTE C. KINNEY [14]

The Heights of Christian Experience

No one could tell me where my soul might be;
I searched for God, and He eluded me;
I sought my brother out, and found all three.
                    —ERNEST CROSBY

SCRIPTURE: Psalms 41:1-2; 46:1-7.

HYMNS: "Rescue the Perishing"; "My Hope Is Built on Nothing Less."

THE STORY:

An American who enjoyed climbing mountains returned time and time again to Switzerland. He was adept at this sport and found no difficulty in getting guides and companions to go with him. Each time he made an ascent there came to him an indescribable joy in the achievement, and he sacrificed much in time, effort, and money to attain the heights.

At first his main difficulty lay in finding someone dependable to do the rough work at the foot of the mountain. But after he secured the hunchbacked boy Luke, his troubles were over. The boy was loyal and helpful and with staunchness stood by at the base as he followed the Alpine climbers with his eyes.

When after a year or so of absence the American returned to Switzerland to make his final climb to the top of the mountain, he found Luke still ready to work for him. As the group was preparing to go to the top, the man turned to the hunchback and asked, "Well, Luke, how would you like to go to the top yourself?"

The poor boy shook his head and looked sadly at his misshapen body.

"I'll see that you get there," vowed the man. And so the party set out. The men had to help Luke most of the way. They climbed slowly but surely and with a will.

When they reached the top of the mountain, their joy was past description as the panorama of the mountains rolled out before them. But they always count it the height of their careers as mountain climbers when Luke, the hunchback, sank to his knees in ecstasy. All he could say was, "O beautiful, beautiful! Thank you, thank you!"

It is a great and wonderful thing to be permitted to climb to the heights—to breath life's rarer atmosphere, to struggle on and up, to stand upon the mount of God with the sunlight in your soul.

But the joy of joys is reached when, standing on the summit, you are able to look around and see another whom you have aided to reach the lofty peak of Christian experience.

COUNT THAT DAY LOST

If you sit down at set of sun
And count the acts that you have done,
And, counting find

57

One self-denying deed, one word
That eased the heart of him who heard;
    One glance most kind,
That fell like sunshine where it went—
Then you may count that day well spent.

But if, through all the livelong day,
You've cheered no heart, by yea or nay—
    If, through it all
You've nothing done that you can trace
That brought the sunshine to one face—
    No act most small
That helped some soul and nothing cost—
Then count that day as worse than lost.
    —GEORGE ELIOT

PRAYER:

To make rough places plain, and crooked straight;
To help the weak; to envy not the strong;
To make the earth a sweeter dwelling place,
In little ways, or if we may, in great,
And in the world to help the heavenly song,
We pray, Lord Jesus, grant to us thy grace! Amen.
    —AUTHOR UNKNOWN

Inspiration

There lives and works a soul in all things,
And that soul is God.

—WILLIAM COWPER

SCRIPTURE: Luke 15:3-10.

HYMNS: "There's a Wideness in God's Mercy"; "The Lord Is My Shepherd."

THE STORY:

Ira Sankey read the poem "The Ninety and Nine" in London in the *Christian Age*. It had been written by Elizabeth Clephane of Scotland, and it so impressed him that he clipped it and carried it in his pocket for many months. Often he would read it, and each time he was impressed anew with its beauty and meaning.

At a very important point in one of their evangelistic meetings Dwight L. Moody turned to him and whispered, "Sing something new!"

Sankey had the very poem in his pocket to suit the occasion, but as yet there was no music written for it. Praying for God's guidance, he brought out the clipping, laid it on the reed organ, and began to play. He sang the words and composed at the same time. The tune grew. He played it again for the second stanza and then for the others. This hymn tune, composed with a thousand people listening, was born of inspiration, consecration, and memory. It is said that the audience heard every word of the poem as he sang and that its message left them in tears.

Sankey testified that it was the most intense moment of his life.

To very few of us is given the opportunity of such a perfect revelation, but day by day we may feel ourselves directed and inspired by our heavenly Father. Trained to seek his will, to listen to his voice, and to consecrate our talents to him, we will be surprised at the result of our humble efforts.

SOLO: "The Ninety and Nine."

PRAYER:

We come, our Father, to seek thee again and again. There is within us that which is not satisfied until we find thee. We comfort ourselves that whatsoever we do, thou canst be with us if we are mindful of thee. Only through thee can we receive true inspiration. As we go about our daily tasks, wilt thou be over us, around us, and within us. So shall we find our fulfillment. Amen.

LO, I AM WITH YOU ALWAYS

Wide fields of corn along the valleys spread;
The rain and dews mature the swelling vine;

I see the Lord is multiplying bread;
  I see him turning water into wine;
  I see him working all the works divine
He wrought when Salemward his steps were led;
  The selfsame miracles around him shine;
He feeds the famished; he revives the dead;

  He pours the flood of light on darkened eyes;
He chases tears, diseases, fiends away;
  His throne is raised upon these orient skies;
His footstool is the pave whereon we pray.
  Ah, tell me not of Christ in Paradise,
For he is all around us here today.

—JOHN CHARLES EARLE

Life's Pattern

'Tis not alone in the sunshine
　Our lives grow pure and true;
There is growth as well in the shadow,
　And pain has a work to do.

So it comes to me more and more
　As I enter upon each new day:
The love of the Father eternal
　Is over us all the way.
　　　　　　—AUTHOR UNKNOWN

SCRIPTURE: Romans 15:1-7.

HYMNS: "In the Hour of Trial"; "O Jesus, I Have Promised."

THE STORY:

There's a rug on my floor. It's a small rug, hand-woven, but is beautiful and natural as something plaited by the wind, sun, and soil. Handmade things have that look, as if something of life itself went into their making. The threads which make up the warp of my rug are blue and gold and brown, and through it runs a woof of foggy gray, heather purple with some vivid flecks of green. This may seem rather scrambled, but actually it is like a bit of woodland carpeting, that rug—now dull as though the colors slept, and then all sparkling with the living light.

I'm foolishly fond of that rug. And yet it moves my heart. Here's why.

There's a certain strangeness in that rug which jolts the soul of anyone who understands its making. The margins are not even; the design has gone astray. Threads are broken; sometimes the colors do not match. Why? Because the weaver of that rug was blind.

All day he sat and wove the woof and warp of scarlet, green, and brown. He had a chart and numbered pegs by which he groped his way. And so he wove within his endless night, building a strip of beauty which his eyes would never see, yet which reflected the hunger in his shadowed soul. Sometimes the weaving went right on as though his fingers held a song. But sometimes he grew weary and indifferent or gave way to despair.

So wove that weaver. So weave you and I. For we too work in darkness which we cannot pierce.

Blindly we come to take our seat beside the loom of life; blindly we leave when night tells us to go. The little laws which other men have built in other days are tags by which we feel our way.

Sometimes the thread is scarlet like a song or gold with love or white with faith and prayer. Sometimes the woof is drab and brown, sullied with our blundering and despair. And often, too, our fingers slip, and all the plan is marred or snarled with angry hands because we cannot see the meaning of it all. And yet, whatever comes, we weave and weave—and weave.

God looks upon this weaving in an altogether different and confident light. He does not weave in the dark. He weaves in love, wisdom, and power.

In the language of the poet the Christian says:

> My life is but a weaving
>   Between my Lord and me;
> I cannot choose the colors
>   He worketh steadily.
>
> Oft times He weaveth sorrow,
>   And I in foolish pride
> Forget He sees the upper
>   And I the under side.
>
> Not till the loom is silent
>   And the shuttles cease to fly,
> Shall God unroll the canvas
>   And explain the reason why.
>
> The dark threads are as needful
>   In the Weaver's skillful hand
> As the threads of gold and silver
>   In the pattern He has planned.[15]

PRAYER:

God our Father, give us grace to praise thee for the difficulties of life. We have learned that life's richest meanings come from those experiences which demand courage and patience. We thank thee for joy and for pain, for the light and for the dark, for the everyday ups and downs of life which make it rich and meaningful. To thee the pattern is evident as we follow in our own imperfect way. Help us to have the steadiness of purpose which will enhance and give detail to the design as we meet our problems bravely. Amen.

SPINNING

Like a blind spinner in the sun,
    I tread my days;
I know that all the threads will run
    Appointed ways;
I know each day will bring its task,
And being blind, no more I ask.
         —HELEN HUNT JACKSON [16]

Mercy

Search thine own heart. What paineth thee
In others in thyself may be;
All dust is frail, all flesh is weak;
Be thou the true man thou dost seek!
—JOHN GREENLEAF WHITTIER

SCRIPTURE: Genesis 2:4-24.

HYMNS: "From Every Stormy Wind That Blows"; "O
Love That Wilt Not Let Me Go."

THE STORY:

"When God was about to create man," say the
rabbis of old, "he called together before his throne a
council of angelic hosts."

"Create him not," said the Angel of Justice, "for
he will be unjust toward his fellow man. He will
injure and oppress the weak and cruelly ill-treat the
feeble."

"Create him not," spoke the Angel of Peace, "for
he will stain the earth with the blood of his brethren;
the first-born of his race will be the murderer of his
brother."

"Create him not," pleaded the Angel of Truth.
"Thou mayest create him in thine image, after thine
own likeness, and even stamp the impress of truth
upon his brow, yet will he desecrate with falsehood
even thine own sanctuary."

Then the Angel of Mercy, the youngest and dearest of the eternal Father, stepped before the sapphire throne and knelt. "Father, O Father, create him, I pray. Create him after thine own image as the favored child of thy goodness. When all others forsake him, I will be with him. I will lovingly aid him and turn his errors to his own good. I will touch his heart with pity and mercy and help him to be kind to others weaker than himself."

And so God listened to the voice of the Angel of Mercy, and he created man.[17]

PRAYER:

O God, who makest all things, we would pray that thy love may grow in our hearts until, moved by a strong sense of the worth of all thy children, we shall be able to be truly merciful and forgiving.

We acknowledge that we have misjudged others and have fallen short in our duty to them and to thee. Strengthen in us a sense of love and devotion for all mankind, that we may more worthily follow thee. Amen.

IF WE KNEW

If we knew the cares and crosses
   Crowding round our neighbor's way,
If we knew the little losses,
   Sorely grievous day by day,
Would we then so often chide him
   For the lack of thrift and gain—

Casting o'er his life a shadow,
  Leaving on his heart a stain?

Let us reach into our bosoms
  For the key to other lives,
And with love to erring nature,
  Cherish good that still survives;
So that when our disrobed spirits
  Soar to realms of light again,
We may say, "Dear Father, judge us
  As we judged our fellow men."
                    —AUTHOR UNKNOWN

Modern Psalms

My heart is a garden, Jehovah the Gardener.
He keeps me from drought; He gives living water;
He provides a hundred kinds of flowers through the four
    seasons;
He surrounds me with fragrance;
The abundant green grass gladdens my heart day by day.
Moreover, the Lord causes the trees of my garden to
    produce fruit;
Fruit for the days to come,
For future generations.

—Ma Hsien-jui [18]

This meditation was written in a garden after the author had read the twenty-third psalm. At that time Ma Hsien-jui was a girl in junior high school; later she became a teacher.

Scripture: Psalm 23.

Hymns: "The Lord Is My Shepherd"; "Saviour, Like a Shepherd Lead Us."

Because of its beauty the twenty-third psalm has been used as a pattern for modern psalms. Mary Dickerson Bangham has written "The Flower Grower's Twenty-Third Psalm":

The Lord is the grower of my flowers;
I shall not want;

69

He rests my tired muscles through the very color
of his green lawns;
He leads me, rested, to the setting out of larkspur;
He restoreth my soul while I plant columbine and
and phlox.
Though the shadow of despair fall upon my garden
path,
I shall not fear.
Thou art with me in sunshine and in shadow;
In my gardening tools I sense thy comforting rod
and thy staff;
Thou preparest a feast of beauty for me in the
presence of a too mechanized world;
From season to season my cup overflows
Its wealth of daffodils and tulips, of pansies and
roses, of marigolds, delphinium, asters, chrysan-
themums.
Hold the balm of thy goodness and of thy mercy;
Sharing thy love and the flowers of the garden
with others,
I find myself already dwelling in thy boundless
and eternal gardens! [19]

PRAYER:

Our Father God, we thank thee that as we feel
thee in our hearts, minds, and spirits, thou dost re-
veal thyself to us. Thou art the Father of all people
of the earth, and each of us interprets thy love and
guidance as he understands it.

May our feet ever be led in the paths of righteous-
ness and peace, as we make our many choices in
life. Amen.

SOLO: "The King of Love My Shepherd Is."

A missionary to the Indians has translated the twenty-third psalm into Indian vernacular:

The Great Father above a Shepherd Chief is the same as, and I am his and with him I want not.

He throws out to me a rope. The name of the rope is Love. He draws me, and draws me, and draws me to where the grass is green and the water not dangerous; and I eat and drink and lie down satisfied.

Some days this soul of mine is very weak and falls down, but he raises it up again and draws me into trails that are good. His name is Wonderful.

Sometime, it may be in a little time, it may be longer and it may be a long, long time, I do not know, he will draw me into a place between mountains. It is dark there but I will pull back not, and I will be afraid not, for it is there, between those mountains, that the Great Shepherd Chief will meet me, and the hunger I have felt in my heart all through this life will be satisfied.

Sometimes the rope that is Love, he makes into a whip and he whips me, and whips me, and whips me but afterward he gives me a staff to lean on.

He spreads a table before me and puts on it different kinds of food; buffalo meat, Chinamen's food, white men's food, and we all sit down and eat that which satisfies us.

He puts his hands on my head and all the "tired" is gone.

He fills my cup till it runs over.

Now, what I am telling you is true. I talk two ways not. These roads that are always "away-ahead-good" will stay with me all through this life, and afterward I will move to the "Big Tepee" and sit down with the Shepherd Chief forever.

—ISABEL CRAWFORD [20]

TRUE LOVE

True love is but a humble, low-born thing,
And hath its food served up in earthenware;
It is a thing to walk with, hand in hand,
Through the everydayness of this work day world.
—JAMES RUSSELL LOWELL

Of One Blood

The world is one; we cannot live apart,
    To earth's remotest races we are kin;
God made the generations of one blood;
Man's separation is a sign of sin.
                    —HINTON WHITE

SCRIPTURE: I Peter 3:8-17.

HYMNS: "In Christ There Is No East or West";
"Take the Name of Jesus with You."

DIFFERENT SKIN

I am the person who is born to live in a skin with a different color from yours. I could not choose my parents, nor you yours.

Thus the color pigments embedded by the unchangeable hands of nature in your skin are perchance white, while mine are black or brown or yellow. But underneath I am just like you.

My muscles ripple in the same ways of power and thrill to the same throb of joyous action.

My mind has the same functions as yours.

I reach out, just as you do, in aspirations of the soul.

I love and hate, hope and despair, rejoice and suffer along with you.

When my children lose their fair chances at life

and become aware of the bitter road of prejudice
they must tread, then I know what my color has cost.
I offer you my hand in rebuilding an unjust world,
that you and I can make better than we found it.
I am the person in a different skin.[21]

> The One bethought Him to make man
>   Of many-colored dust,
> And mixed the Holy Spirit in,
>   In portions right and just;
> Each had a part of mind and heart
>   From One Himself in trust.
>
> Thus came the brown and yellow men,
>   And black and white and red,
> So different in their outer look,
>   Alike in heart and head—
> The self-same dust before their birth,
>   The self-same dust when dead.
>   —PAI TA-SHUN [22]

PRAYER:

Our gracious Father, in the far depths of whose
fatherhood all men were conceived in love and born
to be brothers, we come to thee as thy children. We
thank thee that Jesus in whose heart thou art re-
vealed, teaches us not to confine our service to those
of our own race but to seek out the stranger.

We pray that love may be a world feeling, and
sorrow a world grief, and that thy truth may shine
in all dark places. Amen.

OUTSIDE THE SPECTRUM

Our Heavenly Father must have loved
The colors—every one;
For he scattered them upon the earth
From pastel rainbow spun
Across the dome of Heaven
To the sea's deep changing hue.
He made the brown earth; trees of green;
The summer sky of blue;
The sunset blaze; the afterglow;
The dawn diffused in rising mist;
The mountains' purple aureole;
The morning glories, dewdrop kissed.
But when He looks on man, I think,
He sees but soul and mind;
And where His children are concerned,
Our Father's color blind!

—BESS HAGAMAN TEFFT [23]

Persistence

You will find that luck
Is only pluck
To try things over and over;
Patience and skill,
Courage and will,
Are the four leaves of luck's clover.
—AUTHOR UNKNOWN

SCRIPTURE: II Corinthians 5:6-10.

HYMNS: "Dare to Be Brave, Dare to Be True";
"Truehearted, Wholehearted."

THE STORY:

One day two frogs hopped gaily into the spring-house. Great crocks of milk were placed on low shelves over the cool, bubbling water. Curiosity led the frogs to hop up on the edge of a deep crock of cream, soon to be made into butter.

Losing their balance, they both fell in with a splash. One frog came to the top, swam to the edge of the crock, and finding it was too slippery to climb, sank to the bottom with a "glub, glub."

The other frog, when he came to the surface, swam round and round kicking vigorously for hours and hours. He would not give up.

Strange to relate, when the housewife came to the

76

springhouse for the cream, she found a small pat of butter in the crock, while perched up on top of it was an exhausted frog. But he was alive!

THREE THINGS

Three things I beg of Life to let me keep:
Rare strength, which through dark storm will safely last—
Until my soul's dire need of it is past—
Because its main pilasters reach so deep;
Initiative, with eager, circling sweep
Of wings . . . high courage, of the keen enthusiast
Who even in his dreams can hear the blast
Of trumpet calls that urge him up the steep.
Real strength endures . . . initiative impels,
And flaming courage molds a dauntless heart.
Dynamic power these give—and self-release.
With them, the world's great inner citadels
Are mine . . . gay plumed adventure they impart
To Life—while traveling toward the Sunset Peace.
                              —GERTRUDE B. GUNDERSON

PRAYER:

Our God and Creator, give us the strength to endure which fellowship with thee imparts. Implant in us the unconquered optimism of the Redeemer's faith in man and in thee, O God.

May we know in our small spheres the victory of accomplishment, and may we never be discouraged. Fill us with the conviction that we may depend upon thy spirit in the world and in our lives. Amen.

Prayer

I will not doubt, though all my prayers return
  Unanswered from the still, white realm above;
  I shall believe it is an all-wise Love
Which has refused those things for which I yearn.
            —ELLA WHEELER WILCOX [24]

SCRIPTURE: Hebrews 11:1-3; 12:1-3; Matthew 17: 20-22.

HYMNS: "Blessed Assurance"; "God Is My Strong Salvation."

THE STORY:

When Isabella married Henry Brown, she moved with her husband from the plains into the mountains. Their little cabin lay between two mountains, and in fact Isabella didn't see the sun until mid-morning. As she stood at either her front or her back door, the wooded side of a mountain rose before her eyes.

She felt as if she were hemmed in and as if she were far removed from all she had known.

One evening as she read her Bible a phrase of Jesus' was imprinted upon her mind: "If ye have faith as a grain of mustard seed, ye shall say unto this mountain, Remove hence to yonder place; and it shall remove; and nothing shall be impossible unto you."

"I will pray," she said, "that this mountain at my front door may be removed. But if I pray, I must believe that it will be done."

And so as daily Isabella Brown prayed, always in her prayer was the expressed desire that the mountain at her front door might be removed. She was not impatient, however, and often climbed to the top of it to look at the land beyond—a beautiful valley with a road winding into the distance. In her imagination she removed the mountain and attached the road to her own front-door path. And then she prayed again. "How wonderful it will be!" she thought happily, as she went about her work.

The years passed by, and to Isabella and Henry was born a fine baby boy, and then a lovely, healthy girl. As soon as their little legs were strong enough, they too climbed the mountain and looked over the lovely valley with the beckoning road.

The time came finally when the children were in their teens and would soon be going into town to school. One day as Isabella and her daughter, Jean, sat on the front porch, a group of surveyors came by. They were very busy and scarcely noticed the small cottage. For a week they worked, moving their instruments about and shouting out measurements. As they were leaving, one of the men came to Isabella's door and asked for a drink of water from her spring. "Take all you wish," answered Isabella pleasantly. "It is pure, cool, and plentiful."

Then as the men were leaving, the foreman said,

"You may be glad to know, ma'am, that we are moving our machinery here next week to blast out a section of this mountain. Soon a fine highway will run past your front door."

"Jean," cried Isabella, "did you hear what the man said? Our prayers are answered." Turning to the man, she said, "For years we have prayed that this mountain might be removed. God has answered our prayers in his own way and in his own time. Thank you for being his instrument."

PRAYER:

Father of the spirits of all people, who art ever in the present environment of our lives, we thank thee for thy protecting care. Help us to trust—to have sure faith that thou dost hear our prayers and that thou wilt answer them in thy good time and in the way thou findest best. Amen.

As one who in the valley may abide
  Goes to the hilltop for a rarer air,
So on the heights may I with Thee abide,
  See far horizons, heavens more broad and fair;
And finding life in richer plenitude,
  Nor shackled by the cares from which I flee,
May fill each moment with the sense of good
  Which comes, O Lord, from knowing more of Thee.
          —AUTHOR UNKNOWN

Responsibility

Do thy duty; that is best;
Leave unto thy Lord the rest.
            —James Russell Lowell

Scripture: James 1:22-27.

Hymns: "Be Strong"; "Go, Labor On"; "Hark, the
Voice of Jesus Calling."

The Story:

There is a legend that, when God created the earth
and everything upon it, he gave to every living thing
an angel to watch over it.

The birds, the trees, the deer, the flowers, and even
the vegetables had an angel. He gave an angel charge
of the common grass that grows in the fields.

The angels seemed very happy and worked with
loving care—all except the guardian of the common
grass. This seemed too ordinary a task, and he did
not tend the grass. Deprived of the rain, the sun, and
the air, with which all other growing things were
furnished by the careful ministry of the angels, the
grass soon became yellow and dry.

After a time the angel of the flowers came before
God and explained that, although he had faithfully
tended the flowers, the grass in the meadow did not
get the dew, the air, and the sun it needed. And be-

cause of the lack of care to the grass surrounding them, the flowers withered quickly.

Then the angel of the trees complained because the grass was dry and brittle and the ground was caked and hard around the trees.

The angels of the deer, cattle, and other animals came before God saying there was no green grass for the creatures to eat. The world was fast becoming a desert place.

Then God looked around and saw the angel of the common grass standing disconsolately to one side.

"Do you think your task is too small now?" he asked.

The angel fell down before the throne in sorrow. "O God!" he cried. "You gave me a great task—far greater than I deserved. It was I who was small, petty, and complaining. Try me again, and I will gladly do my part."

So the grass grew, the trees extended their roots and branches, the flowers bloomed, the animals were fed, and all the angels were happy.

There is no task which is common; all duties are important in the sight of the heavenly Father.[25]

YOUR MISSION

If you cannot on the ocean
   Sail among the swiftest fleet,
Rocking on the highest billows,
   Laughing at the storms you meet,
You can stand among the sailors,
   Anchored yet within the bay;

You can lend a hand to help them,
  As they launch their boats away.

If you are too weak to journey
  Up the mountain, steep and high,
You can stand within the valley,
  While the multitude go by;
You can chant in happy measure,
  As they slowly pass along;
Though they may forget the singer,
  They will not forget the song.

If you have not gold and silver
  Ever ready to command,
If you cannot toward the needy
  Reach an ever-open hand,
You can visit the afflicted,
  O'er the erring you can weep;
You can be a true disciple,
  Sitting at the Saviour's feet.

If you cannot be the watchman,
  Standing high on Zion's wall,
Pointing out the path to heaven,
  Offering life and peace to all,
With your prayers and with your bounties
  You can do what Heaven demands;
You can be a faithful Aaron,
  Holding up the prophet's hands.

Do not then stand idly waiting
  For some greater work to do;
Fortune is a lazy goddess,
  She will never come to you.
Go and toil in any vineyard,
  Do not fear to do or dare;

If you want a field of labor,
You can find it anywhere.
—ELLEN M. H. GATES

PRAYER:

Almighty Father, we give thee praise for this day. Thou dost watch over thy creatures with loving care.

Graciously help us to abide in thee and be strong and steadfast. Thy light hath never failed us, nor hath thy grace ever left us. May our coming days be filled with a sense of mission, and may our remembrance of thy patient love and care deliver us from waywardness and from the neglect of our responsibilities. Amen.

Service

Go make thy garden fair as thou canst—
    Thou workest never alone;
Perchance he whose plot is next to thine
    Will see it, and mend his own.
                —ELIZABETH RUNDLE CHARLES

SCRIPTURE: Hebrews 1:8-14.

HYMNS: "How Gentle God's Commands"; "Sun of My Soul."

THE STORY:

I had noticed for several days, as I took my country walk, an old man who was gathering up stones which he put into a small sack. When this sack was a quarter full, he swung it, with evident effort, across his shoulder and limped away leaning on a stout stick. I saw him enter a short cart road which led to a little farm.

A moment later a robust young man, who had a good-natured face, came out from this lane, and I ventured to ask what the old man gathered stones for.

"Oh! Old Granddad!" he exclaimed with a loud laugh. "I'll show you, ma'am. You can see two lines all up this road of a lighter color than the road; Granddad has filled up two deep ruts, carrying a few stones at a time, because he thinks the old mare found

85

the ruts made her load harder to draw. He has been two months at it and must be about finished. It amuses him and does no harm, though I must say I can't see the good of it."

The old man heard the last part of this speech, for he had come up the lane as he emptied the sack into the last bit of rut. He looked up, smiling as he said, "So you don't see the good of it? Well, the old mare thinks different."

Then, turning toward me, he said, "That mare and me are old. We know it's some good to have rough places made smooth!"

I heartily agreed with him. We have every day countless chances of making rough places smooth for others, and there is no surer way of smoothing our own path.[26]

> Who gives, and hides the giving hand,
>   Nor counts on favor, fame, or praise,
>   Shall find his smallest gift outweighs
> The burden of the sea and land.
>
>
> Who gives to whom hath naught been given,
>   His gift in need, though small indeed
>   As is the grass-blade's wind-blown seed,
> Is large as earth and rich as heaven.
>   —JOHN GREENLEAF WHITTIER

PRAYER:

Dear Father, we thank thee for all faithful souls who have given their lives to the service of mankind and especially for the humble ones who have smoothed the way for others yet unborn.

May we recognize true greatness in all places and may we in humility participate in the sacrifice and tireless effort of the many unnamed ones of the earth. We thank thee for this privilege. Amen.

THE TOUCH OF HUMAN HANDS

The touch of human hands—
That is the boon we ask;
For groping, day by day,
Along the stony way,
We need the comrade heart
That understands,
And the warmth, the living warmth
Of human hands.

The touch of human hands;
Not vain, unthinking words,
Nor that cold charity
Which shuns our misery;
We seek a loyal friend
Who understands,
And the warmth, the pulsing warmth
Of human hands.

The touch of human hands—
Such care as was in him

Who walked in Galilee
Beside the silver sea;
We need a patient guide
Who understands,
And the warmth, the loving warmth
Of human hands.

—THOMAS CURTIS CLARK [27]

Thanksgiving

Were thanks with every gift expressed,
  Each day would be Thanksgiving;
Were gratitude its very best,
  Each life would be thanksliving.
                    —CHAUNCEY R. PIETY [28]

SCRIPTURE: Psalms 105:1-5; 111:1-9.

HYMNS: "Come, Ye Thankful People, Come"; "For the Beauty of the Earth"; "America the Beautiful."

THE STORY:

Constanta White was very busy at her household tasks. There was much for a young Pilgrim wife to do in those first years in Plymouth. To be sure, her life had never been easy, but always there had been plenty of food and clothes. Now her task was to supply her beloved husband with the sustenance he needed. It required strength on his part to help lift the heavy logs and hew the timbers for the building program the governor had ordered. Constanta and her husband had but one corner of a big log building to call their home. Many families were living there until their houses were built.

Just now she looked at a handful of coarse meal and the remainder of a wild fowl her husband had killed. Then she took a pinch of seasoning from a small box which she had brought from her home across the seas. "At least this is familiar," she thought as she smiled to herself. Her heart grew light as she fashioned a small meat pie for dinner.

The days of summer sped fast. The men occasionally fished for cod and bass and dug for clams, to vary the food of the colony. One day a flock of large fowl flew over the village, and the men stopped work long enough to shoot some of them. They were the first wild turkeys they had seen and were a welcome delicacy.

In the autumn some friendly Indians brought handfuls of grain which they called maize. Constanta and the other matrons learned from these new friends how to dry the corn and to grind it into meal.

One day as she counted the many blessings which were hers, and the many instances of God's loving care, Constanta's heart seemed full to overflowing with thankfulness. All day she hummed and thought as she walked lightly about the little log cabin recently assigned to her and Edward White.

That night she spoke to her husband with deep earnestness, "Edward, we have been so busy providing the necessities of life that we have not given proper thought to the part God has played in our blessings, nor have we been sufficiently grateful to our friends the Indians. Should we not have a day of thankfulness, rejoicing, and reverence?"

"My dear Constanta," he replied, "I will ask the governor what he thinks."

And so as the food was gathered in and as the month of November came near, Governor Bradford issued a proclamation. No one knew that the idea of the first Thanksgiving may have sprung up in the heart and mind of a brave, loving little woman who recognized the hand of God in all things and who was thankfully willing to share her blessings.

A WOMAN COUNTS HER BLESSINGS

Strange how Thanksgiving means so much to me
This year! And yet perhaps not strange because
I stole an hour from out the day to pause
And estimate my blessings prayerfully.
I'd been subtracting only woes before,
Where on life's slate were many joys to add,
And when I tallied these, I found I had
A total startling-precious in its score.

Ah, how insidious, self-pity! Poor?
I, with a roof for shelter, food, and health?
A husband, children, friends—in them a sure
Trust fund of love? And all of beauty's wealth?

So now I go about my work on wings,
While, "Thank you, thank you, thank you!" my heart
    sings.

—ETHEL ROMIG FULLER [29]

PRAYER:

With our whole heart we give thee thanks, our Father, for the gifts of faith and hope that make for happiness around us and within us, for the light of knowledge, for the discipline of duty, for the ties and obligations of kindred, and for our knowledge of thy great and tender mercies.

At this special time of Thanksgiving may we acknowledge fully thy great gifts and pledge ourselves anew in loyalty to the Christian way. Amen.

The Tongue

Boys flying kites haul in their white-winged birds,
You can't do that when you're flying words.
Careful with fire is good advice, we know;
Careful with words is ten times doubly so.
Thoughts unexpressed sometimes fall back dead,
But God himself can't kill them once they're said.
—WILL CARLETON [30]

SCRIPTURE: James 3:1-10; Proverbs 20:17-19.

HYMNS: "Take Time to Be Holy"; "I Want a Principle Within."

THE STORY:

Assuma was an Algonquin chieftain and as wise as he was good.

One day a young girl came to him and confessed that she had told a falsehood about another girl of whom she was jealous. She wept and asked what she could do to recall the words she had spread about.

"At dawn you shall go with me to the top of the high hill," he answered. "You must bring a large goose with you. I shall be waiting for you."

The chief sent word to all the members of the tribe to assemble at the foot of the hill the next morning at dawn.

93

The sad young girl came bringing the goose to Assuma at the appointed time and place. He grasped the fowl firmly and plucked a feather from its wing. Holding it high in the air, he threw the feather from him. It was caught by the breeze and whirled away.

"My daughter," said Assuma, "you shall stand in this spot and pick the feathers from the goose, one by one, setting them adrift in the wind. When all are plucked, join us at the foot of the hill."

All through the day the maiden plucked the feathers one by one. At evening she came down the hill to her people.

"My children," said Assuma, "you have witnessed the scattering of feathers through the day. It is like words drifting here and there on the winds of speech. You alone can find them. Tomorrow you shall seek the feathers which this maiden has plucked. For each feather there shall be a reward. When evening comes, we shall gather again to rejoice that the good name of one of our girls has been restored."

The Indians searched all day. At evening only eight feathers had been found. Assuma gave these to the weeping girl. "Take these feathers to the girl whom you have wronged," said the chief. "Tell her that these eight feathers are all you can give to her, as you restore her good name."

And so a great truth was taught to the Algonquin tribe—and to you and to me.

THREE THINGS COME NOT BACK

Remember three things come not back:
The arrow sent upon its track—
It will not swerve, it will not stay
Its speed; it flies to wound, or slay.
The spoken word so soon forgot
By thee; but it has perished not;
In other hearts 'tis living still
And doing work for good or ill.
And the lost opportunity
That cometh back no more to thee.
In vain thou weepest, in vain dost yearn,
Those three will nevermore return.
—FROM THE ARABIAN

PRAYER:

Our Father, help us to guard our tongues from expressing in haste and malice those words which should never be uttered. Help us to create within ourselves a spirit of understanding and good will which will render impossible even uncharitable and unkind thoughts.

May we remember that charity begets charity and that the world gives us back the attitude which we ourselves show.

O that mine eyes might closèd be
To what concerns me not to see;
That deafness might possess mine ear
To what concerns me not to hear;
That truth my tongue might always tie
From ever speaking foolishly. Amen.
—THOMAS ELLWOOD

Unselfishness

Slightest actions often meet the sorest needs,
For the world wants daily little kindly deeds.
                    —Author Unknown

Scripture: Matthew 16:24-28.

Hymns: "Walk in the Light"; "He Leadeth Me."

The Story:

The story is told of a wealthy man who had three nephews but no sons. He wished to leave the main responsibility for his business to the boy who was most able to carry it. One day he asked all three to come to his office.

"One of you will be my successor," he said. "I shall give you each a coin. This large room must be filled with something purchased with the coin. You must fill the room as full as you can but spend no more money than this amount. Return this evening, and I shall be waiting."

After thanking him for his trust in them, the young men departed their separate ways and made their purchases.

At evening the man was met by the boys. The first youth had bought two huge bales of straw, which filled half of the room. The second youth had bought two bags of thistledown which when released flew everywhere but, when it had settled, filled only three fourths of the room.

The third youth stood sadly by. "And what did you purchase?" inquired his uncle.

"I gave half of my coin to a hungry child," he answered, "and most of the rest to the church where I knelt to pray. And then with the few cents I had left I purchased these matches and a tall candle." With these words he lit the candle, and the light filled every corner of the room.

"You alone have caused the room to be filled," said the old man approvingly. The young man fell to his knees as the old man blessed him and made him his successor.

A PRAYER

Dear God, the light is come, our outgrown creeds
Drop from us as a garment, and our sight
Grows clear to see ourselves and Thee aright;
We trust our love to meet our utmost needs,
And know Thy hand sustains us. The foul breeds
Of nameless doubts and fears that thronged the night
Like phantoms disappear in Truth's clear light;
Self only, now our upward way impedes:
For Thou hast given new bottles for Truth's wine:
Hast given a larger faith to help us live
A larger life; new knowledge that will give
A lamp to lead us on to the divine:
And though our feet may falter in the way,
Yet shall our eyes behold Love's Perfect Day!
                              —AUTHOR UNKNOWN

PRAYER:

Our heavenly Father, we would know more of the simple joys of life. In this age of complexity and materialism may we find solutions to our problems in the faith that thou wilt lead us in the paths of wisdom. Although human relationships seem complicated and involved, may we trust to thy leadership simply and lovingly.

Help us to be more like our Lord and Master. Enlarge the capacity of our hearts and illumine our minds. Amen.

Vision

Teach me the faith of the mountains, their strength to
    to endure—
The breadth and the depth of their vision, unswerving
    and sure.

—Author Unknown

Scripture: Matthew 10:39; Philippians 3:8-15.

Hymns: "O Sometimes the Shadows Are Deep"; "He
    Leadeth Me."

The Story:

A man had three sons, and he wished to find out
how enduring their power and vision were. Pointing
into the distance one morning, he said, "My sons,
I'm asking you to go across the mountains as far as
you can, and each of you must bring to me whatever
you consider the greatest treasure."

The sons started out together eagerly to do their
father's bidding.

At the end of the first day one son came back
carrying a beautiful flower. The father thanked him,
but he knew the mountains and could guess where the
flower had been picked.

At the end of the second day another son came
home with a stone of rugged beauty. The father
thanked him and knew by the type of stone how
far this boy had gone.

At the end of the third day the other son did not appear, and as he had not returned at the end of the fourth day, a searching party was sent out.

They found that he had ascended to the top of the highest mountain and, while standing on a crag, had fallen into a crevasse, where he lay wounded.

After rescuing him they brought him to his father, who asked, "And what have you brought to me, my son?"

"Oh, father, standing on the peak of the mountain and looking as it seemed over the whole world, I had a vision. And as I rose on tiptoe to meet it, I forgot myself and, losing my footing, fell."

"You are my wisest son," commended the father. "For the sake of your vision you lost yourself. 'He that loseth his life for my sake shall find it,' are the words of our Saviour."

THE LURE OF THE UNATTAINED

It is easy to foot the trodden path
    Where thousands walked before,
It is simple to push my fragile bark
    Past the reefs of a charted shore.

I find it good to ride the road
    Where others laid the rail.
It is well to test the ocean's strength
    Where others also sail.

But when a dream enslaves a man,
    A dream of the vast untrod,

A dream that says, "Strike out with me,
   Strike out or part with God,"

A dream that leads to an untried path
   Where unknown tempests blow,
And the only chart a man can boast
   Is the will that bids him go,

Ah, then, my soul, bethink yourself,
   For God has spread this scroll
To test the stuff of your rough-hewn faith
   And the fiber of your soul.
                        —PERCY R. HAYWARD [31]

PRAYER:

   Dear Father—
   Teach me the faith of the mountains,
         Serene and sublime,
   The deep-rooted joy of just living
         One day at a time,
   Leaving the petty possessions
         The valley folk buy
   For the glory of glad wind-swept spaces,
         Where earth mets the sky. Amen.
                        —AUTHOR UNKNOWN

101

We Are the Light

O Light serene and still!
Come and our spirits fill,
    Bring in the day:
Guide of our feeble sight,
Star of our darkest night,
Shine on the path of right,
    Show us the way!
            —KING ROBERT OF FRANCE

SCRIPTURE: Ephesians 5:1-14; Matthew 5:14-16.

HYMNS: "Lead Kindly Light"; "O Love That Wilt Not Let Me Go."

THE STORY:

Many years ago an American woman who loved the byways of Europe found herself in a small village between Saxony and Bohemia.

She entered the village on foot, alpenstock in hand and a small kit of necessities upon her back. She was somewhat out of breath from the steep incline of the path and sat down to rest on a flat rock by the wayside.

The magnificent sunset was dying in the west, and the ruins of a medieval castle were silhouetted on the crag of a towering mountain.

In the midst of the short and narrow streets was a paved square, surrounded by small shops and a primi-

102

tive inn. A flight of worn stone steps led up to a
church built or roughhewn stone.

As the woman sat, lights began to gleam in the
windows of the cottages. She made her way to the inn,
knowing that she would find it clean. There would be
a high feather bed covered with coarse homespun
linen. For food she would have a thick vegetable soup,
brown bread, and cheese made from goat's milk. She
had her own tea and loaf sugar.

She was greeted kindly by the innkeeper's wife.
"Madam has come to see the castle! Martin Luther
once visited here. This village is Lutheran from the
time of the Great Elector of Saxony."

After supper the traveler went to her room over-
looking the square. The church bell was ringing for
service, and out from the narrow streets came people,
each bearing a quaint little object which she could
not at first identify. As she peered more closely, she
saw that the objects were iron or bronze lamps of
ancient Roman design—oil lamps with wicks, such as
the wise and foolish virgins might have carried.

The church bell was ringing, but at first only the
steps of the church were lighted. Then, as she
watched, a faint glow gradually outlined the long
windows. She was drawn down the stairs and out into
the street by the music of a chorale, solemn, high,
and sweet.

As she followed along in a steady stream of church-
goers, each bearing a lamp, a woman came abreast of
her. She was late and hurried.

The traveler could not restrain her curiosity and, begging her pardon, accosted the woman, saying, "I am a stranger. Please tell me why you carry a lamp to church."

"Won't you walk along with me?" the woman said. "You see, there is no other way of lighting our church. It is a very old custom in this village, for when the duke who lived in the castle in 1550 built the church, he endowed it and put into writing his wish that the folk should each bring his or her own lamp. He even furnished the lamps, and the church loans them to the families year by year. We have never departed from the custom."

"Does it not keep the people from attending the evening service?"

"Oh, no! It works the other way! You see, it is called 'The Church of the Lighted Lamps.' Everybody that goes makes it a little brighter, and when a body is tempted to take her ease and stay at home, a body remembers that the church needs everybody's lamp, and if your lamp isn't there, there's so much less light. We light our lamps at the torch on the steps and set them in the sockets of the bookracks in each pew. You see, we each have our very own place, and one is missed if one stays away. And then one misses the blessing! We need it to tide us over the week."

From the small table at the entrance she handed a lamp to the traveler. They entered softly, and the woman moved forward to her own pew while the guest was motioned to another. Her seat was in the shadow until she placed her lamp. Then she noted that under each socket was a name. She herself was the guest of one of the daughters of the ancient duke.

As she saw that the many lighted lamps illuminated the names of the faithful who were present, she thought of a line from Scripture, "He calleth his own sheep by name," and again, "The Lord knoweth them that are his." [32]

> God's candles we—
> Some burning high, some low.
> We see the flames as souls
> Where'er we go.
>
> God's candles we—
> If set where dark or light,
> It matters not if we but keep
> His altars bright.
>
> God's candles we—
> Lit from his radiant flame;
> If we burn clear and high,
> We glorify his name.
>
> God's candles we—
> Oh, may we brighter glow
> To lighten other flames
> That flicker low.
>
> —GRACE FOSTER [33]

PRAYER:

Father of light, we come to thee, seeking not only to reflect thy radiance but to become ourselves carriers of light to a darkened world. May we ever carry the light of Christ-consciousness in our souls. Help us to be loving and humble enough to be worthy of thy statement, "Ye are the light of the world." Amen.

REFERENCES

1. "The Rotten Apple in the Sound Barrel," by Glenn Clark. By permission of the author.
2. By permission of Houghton Mifflin Co.
3. From "True Brotherhood." By permission of W. B. Conkey Co.
4. "Alabaster Cruse" from *Holy Flame*, published by Bruce Humphries, Inc. By permission of Georgia Harkness.
5. By permission of Madeleine Sweeney Miller.
6. "The Golden Windows," by Laura E. Richards. Copyright 1903 by Little, Brown & Co. Reprinted by permission of the trustee u/w Laura E. Richards.
7. From *Including Finnigin*, published by Forbes & Co. By permission of Strickland W. Gillilan.
8. "Shallow Water." By permission of *The Christian Herald*.
9. From *Music and Other Poems* by Henry van Dyke. Copyright 1904 by Charles Scribner's Sons, 1932 by Henry van Dyke. Used by permission of the publishers.
10. Adapted from "Timberline," by Cyrus E. Albertson. By permission of the *Christian Advocate*.
11. By permission of Leonora Speyer.
12. "Summary." By permission of Beulah Frances Holland.
13. Adapted from "And Let the Glory Out" in *There Are Sermons in Stories*, by William L. Stidger. By permission of Abingdon-Cokesbury Press.
14. By permission of the *Christian Advocate*.
15. From the newspaper column "Listen, World," by Elsie Robinson. Reprinted by permission of King Features Syndicate, Inc. The poem is quoted from an unknown source.
16. By permission of Little, Brown & Co.
17. Adapted from the Babylonian Talmud.
18. "A Chinese Psalm." By permission of *World Outlook*.
19. From *The Church School*. Copyright 1947 by Pierce & Smith. By permission of the author.
20. By permission of Isabel Crawford.
21. A classic by an unknown writer.

22. From *Bound in the Bundle of Life,* by Margaret T. Applegarth. By permission of Harper & Bros.
23. By permission of Bess Hagaman Tefft.
24. From "Faith." By permission of W. B. Conkey Co.
25. Adapted from "You Are Important to God," by Viola Merritt Lyle. By permission of *Clear Horizons.*
26. Adapted from "Making Rough Places Smooth," by Mrs. Coulson Kernahan. By permission of the *Christian Advocate.*
27. By permission of Thomas Curtis Clark.
28. "Thanksliving." By permission of Chauncey R. Piety.
29. By permission of Ethel Romig Fuller.
30. From "The First Settler's Story" in *Farm Festivals,* by Will Carleton.
31. By permission of the *International Journal of Religious Education.*
32. Adapted from *The Church of the Lighted Lamps,* by Elizabeth Cheney. By permission of Abingdon-Cokesbury Press.
33. By permission of Grace Foster.